Jack And The Beanstalk

Once upon a time, there lived a widow who had a son named Jack. She was very poor and Jack was too young to work. Almost all the furniture of their little cottage had been sold to buy food. At last, there was nothing left to sell. Only the good cow, Milky White, remained. She gave milk every morning. But, one day, Milky White gave no milk, and then, things looked bad indeed.

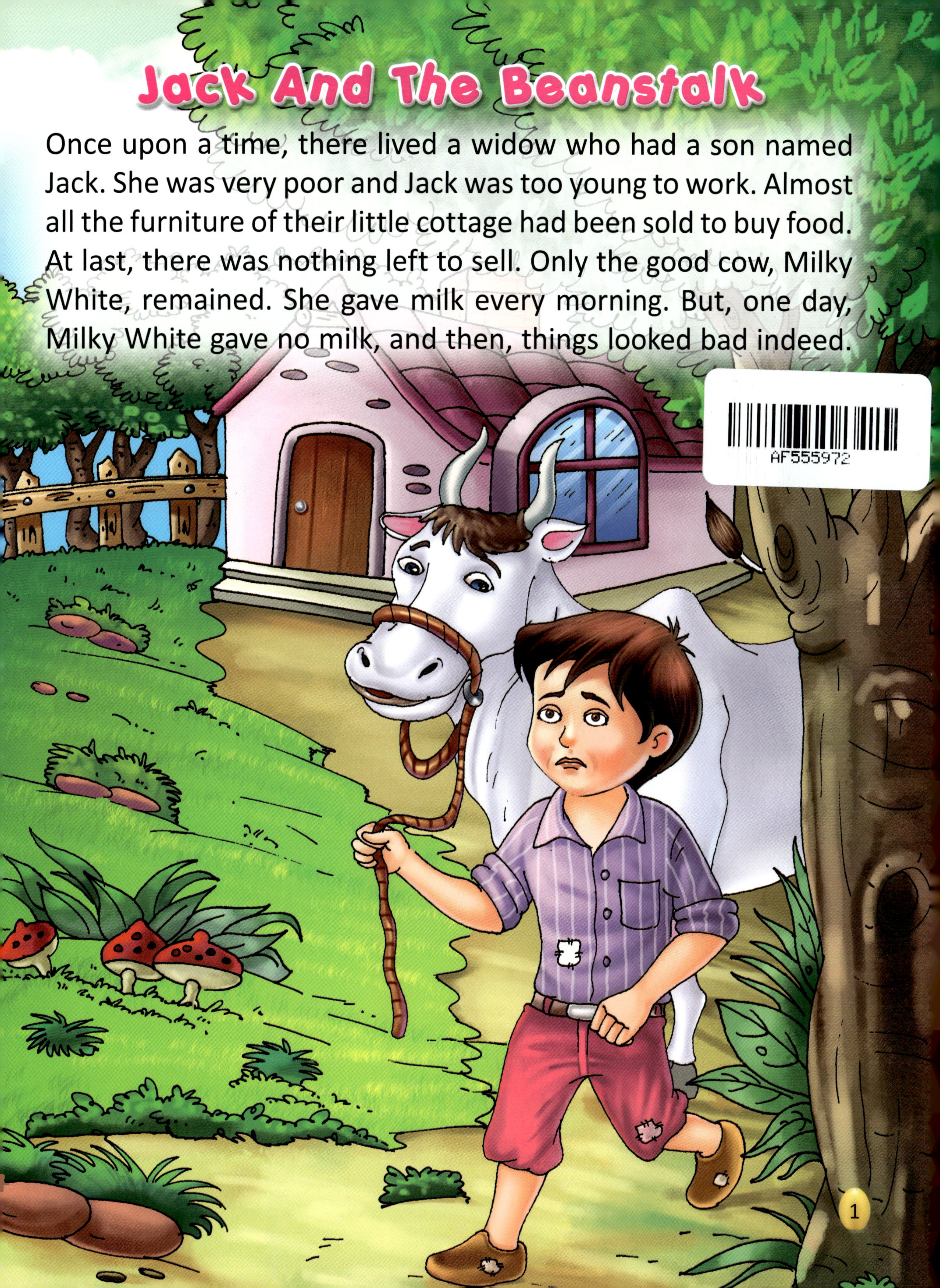

AF555972

"Don't worry, Mother," said Jack, "We shall sell Milky White. You must trust me to make a good bargain." Saying so, he left for the market with the cow.

On the way, he met a butcher. The butcher said, "You can sell this cow to me for these five magic beans. Plant them tonight, and by tomorrow morning, they'll grow up and reach the sky. Climb the beanstalk and you shall find your fortune there."

Jack was so delighted with the bargain that he ran all the way home to tell his mother how lucky he had been. But, his mother was extremely furious at his stupidity.

In a rage, she threw the beans out of the window into the garden, and sent poor Jack to bed without any supper.

When Jack woke up the next morning, the room was almost dark. He jumped out of bed and went to the window to see what had happened as the Sun was shining brightly on the other side. His mouth opened wide at what he saw. From the ground, right up beside his window, grew a huge beanstalk. It stretched up and up, as far as he could see into the sky.

"I'll just see where it leads to," thought Jack curiously and with that, he stepped out of the window onto the beanstalk, and began to climb upwards. He climbed up and up till his mother's cottage looked a mere speck below. At last, the stalk ended, and he found himself standing in front of a grand castle. The castle was huge and had very high walls. The gate of the castle was grand and seemed to be made of gold.

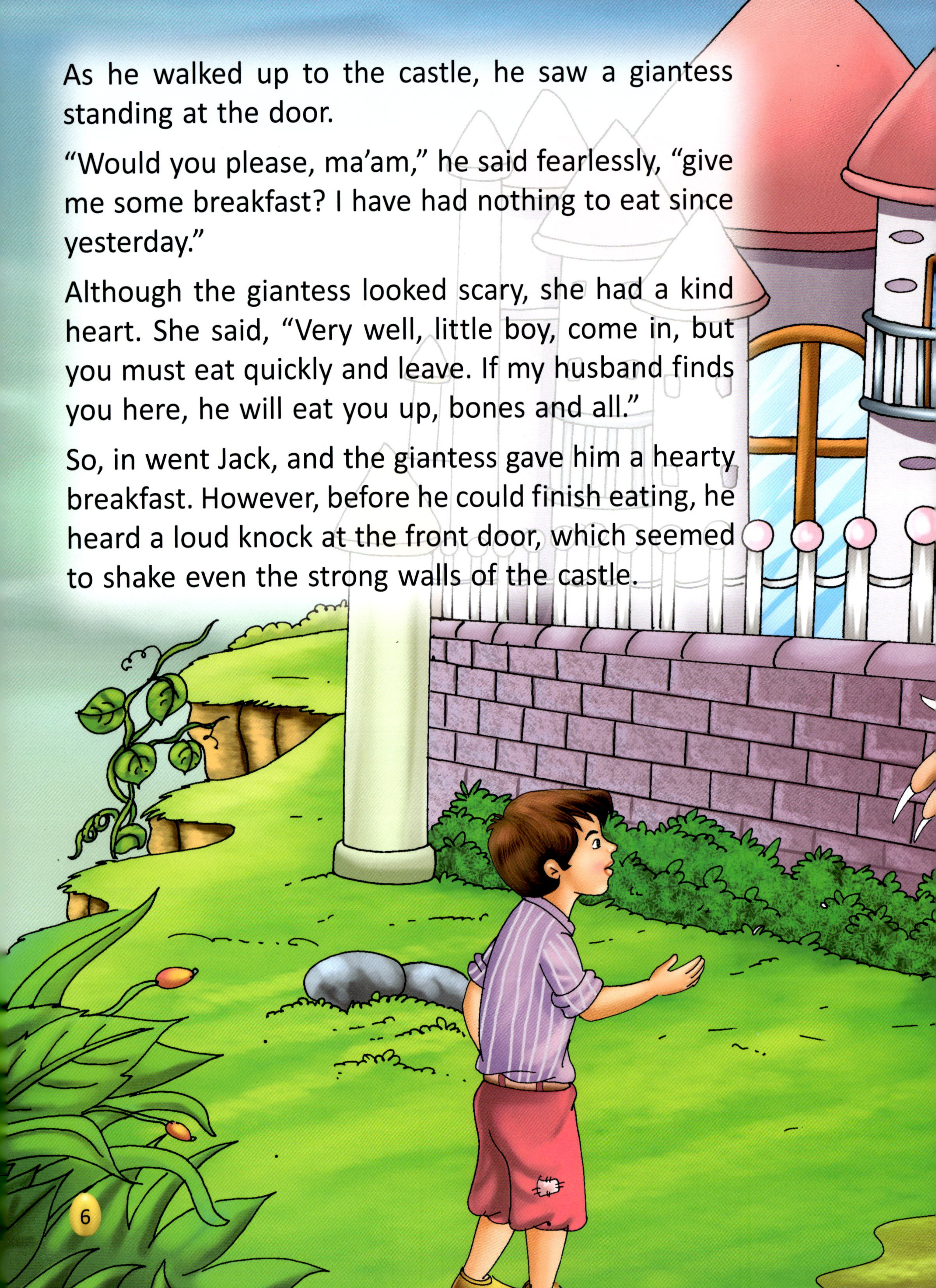

As he walked up to the castle, he saw a giantess standing at the door.

"Would you please, ma'am," he said fearlessly, "give me some breakfast? I have had nothing to eat since yesterday."

Although the giantess looked scary, she had a kind heart. She said, "Very well, little boy, come in, but you must eat quickly and leave. If my husband finds you here, he will eat you up, bones and all."

So, in went Jack, and the giantess gave him a hearty breakfast. However, before he could finish eating, he heard a loud knock at the front door, which seemed to shake even the strong walls of the castle.

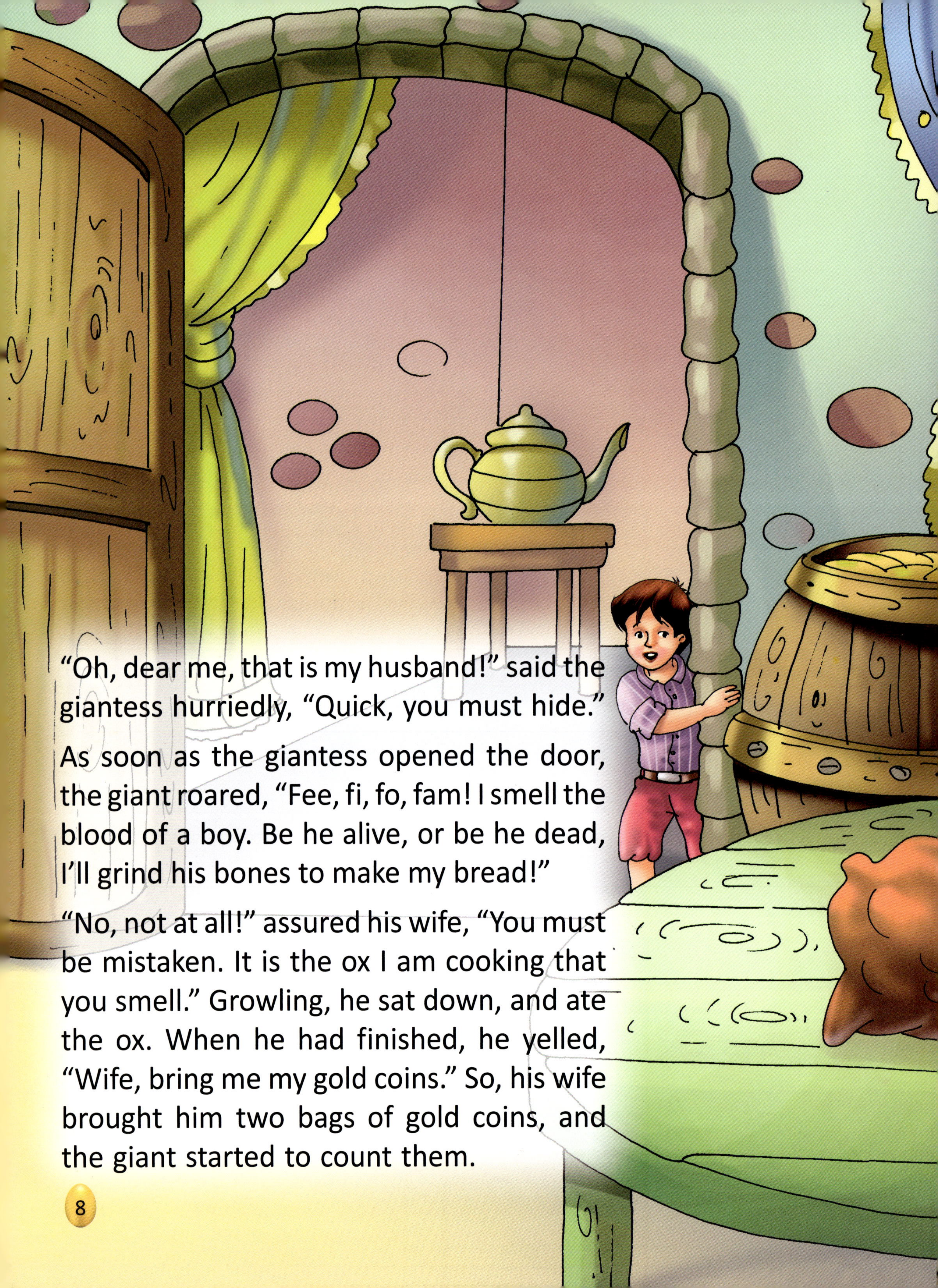

"Oh, dear me, that is my husband!" said the giantess hurriedly, "Quick, you must hide."

As soon as the giantess opened the door, the giant roared, "Fee, fi, fo, fam! I smell the blood of a boy. Be he alive, or be he dead, I'll grind his bones to make my bread!"

"No, not at all!" assured his wife, "You must be mistaken. It is the ox I am cooking that you smell." Growling, he sat down, and ate the ox. When he had finished, he yelled, "Wife, bring me my gold coins." So, his wife brought him two bags of gold coins, and the giant started to count them.

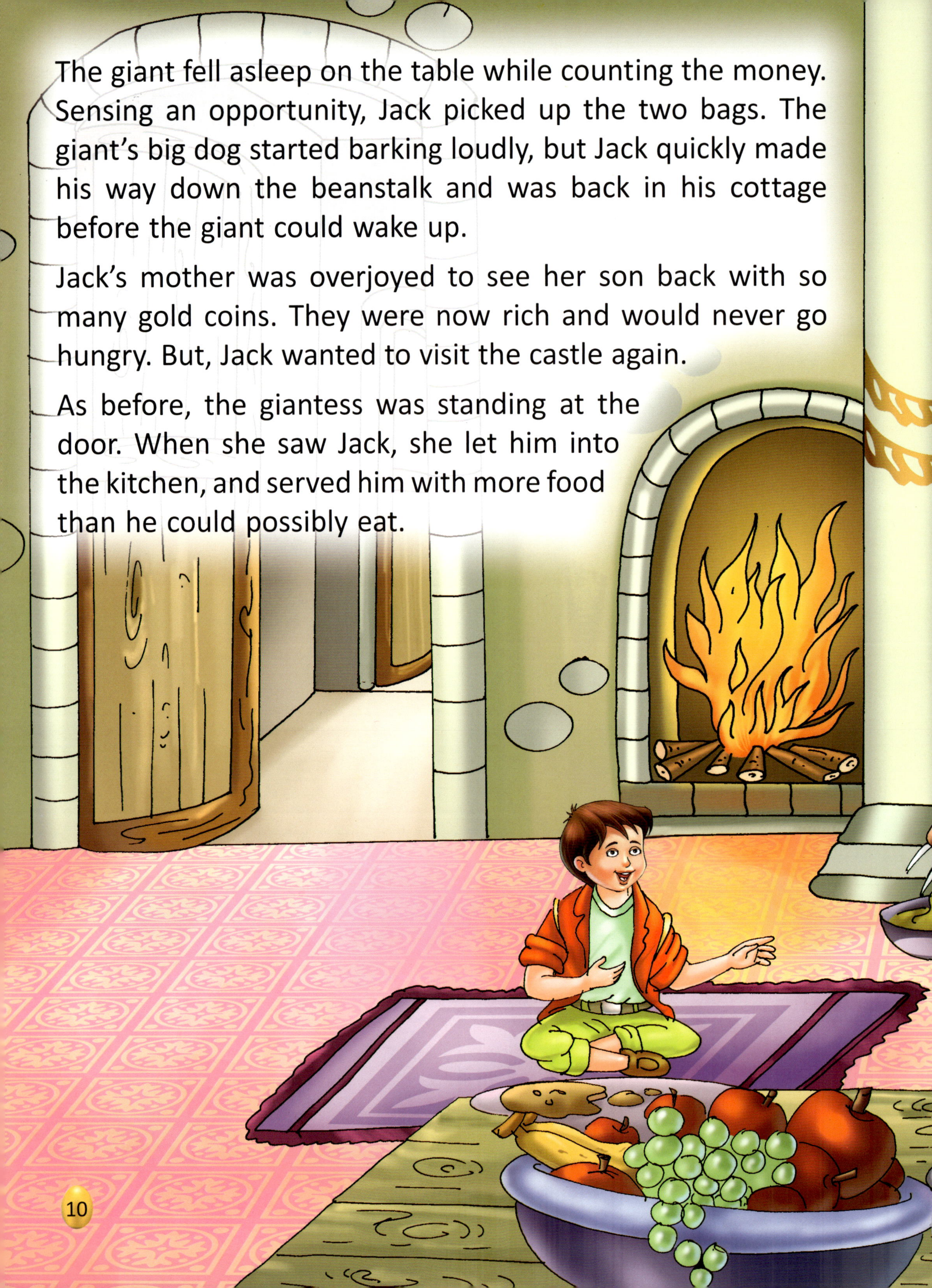

The giant fell asleep on the table while counting the money. Sensing an opportunity, Jack picked up the two bags. The giant's big dog started barking loudly, but Jack quickly made his way down the beanstalk and was back in his cottage before the giant could wake up.

Jack's mother was overjoyed to see her son back with so many gold coins. They were now rich and would never go hungry. But, Jack wanted to visit the castle again.

As before, the giantess was standing at the door. When she saw Jack, she let him into the kitchen, and served him with more food than he could possibly eat.

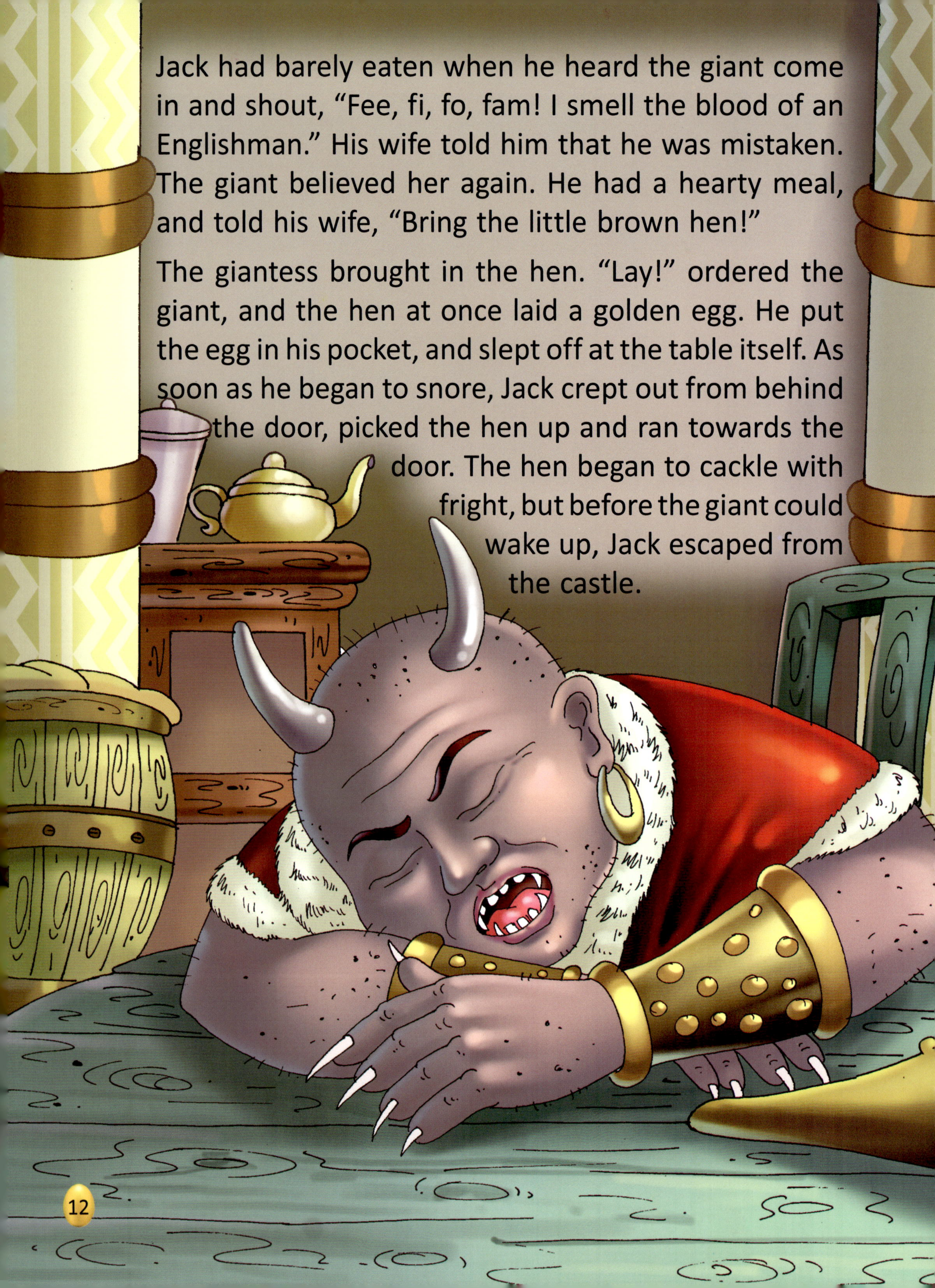

Jack had barely eaten when he heard the giant come in and shout, “Fee, fi, fo, fam! I smell the blood of an Englishman.” His wife told him that he was mistaken. The giant believed her again. He had a hearty meal, and told his wife, “Bring the little brown hen!”

The giantess brought in the hen. “Lay!” ordered the giant, and the hen at once laid a golden egg. He put the egg in his pocket, and slept off at the table itself. As soon as he began to snore, Jack crept out from behind the door, picked the hen up and ran towards the door. The hen began to cackle with fright, but before the giant could wake up, Jack escaped from the castle.

The little brown hen laid so many golden eggs that Jack and his mother now had more money than they could spend.

But, Jack wanted to visit the castle one last time to try his luck. This time, he was careful not to be seen. He crept to the back entrance of the castle and hid himself in the huge oven.

When the giant came in, he roared, "Fee, fi, fo, fam! I smell the blood of an Englishman."

But, the giantess was quite sure that she had seen no little boys that morning. After grumbling a great deal, the giant sat down for breakfast. When he had finished eating, he said to his wife, "Bring me the golden harp." The giantess brought in the golden harp, and placed it on the table.

"Sing!" ordered the giant, and the harp at once began to sing the most melodious songs that were ever heard. It sang so sweetly that the giant soon fell fast asleep.

Grabbing the opportunity, Jack crept quietly out of the oven, and tiptoed to the table to seize the golden harp.

But the harp at once called out, "Master! Master!" The giant woke up just in time to catch sight of Jack running out of the kitchen door.

With a terrible roar, he seized his club and dashed after Jack, who held the harp tight and ran faster than he had ever run before. The giant, waving his club, and taking terribly long strides, gained on Jack with every step. But luckily for Jack, the giant tripped on a stone and fell down.

Before he could stand up, Jack began to climb down the beanstalk. By the time the giant reached the beanstalk, Jack had nearly reached the bottom of the beanstalk.

Jack got hold of an axe and quickly chopped the beanstalk down. The giant crashed down to the ground with a terrible sound, and that was the very end of the mighty giant.

The hen continued laying golden eggs every day. Jack and his mother always had plenty to eat. They listened to the sweet songs of the harp, and lived happily ever after.

Printed in India